SAVING THE ENDANGERED
GREEN SEA TURTLE

SARAH MACHAJEWSKI

Britannica
Educational Publishing

IN ASSOCIATION WITH

ROSEN
EDUCATIONAL SERVICES

Published in 2016 by Britannica Educational Publishing (a trademark of Encyclopædia Britannica, Inc.) in association with The Rosen Publishing Group, Inc.
29 East 21st Street, New York, NY 10010

Distributed exclusively by Rosen Publishing.
To see additional Britannica Educational Publishing titles, go to rosenpublishing.com.

First Edition

Britannica Educational Publishing
J.E. Luebering: Director, Core Reference Group
Mary Rose McCudden: Editor, Britannica Student Encyclopedia

Rosen Publishing
Christine Poolos: Editor
Nelson Sá: Art Director
Michael Moy: Designer
Cindy Reiman: Photography Manager
Carina Finn: Photo Researcher

Library of Congress Cataloging-in-Publication Data

Machajewski, Sarah.
Saving the endangered green sea turtle / Sarah Machajewski.
    pages cm. — (Conservation of endangered species)
Includes bibliographical references and index.
Audience: Grades 1 to 4.
ISBN 978-1-68048-251-5 (library bound) — ISBN 978-1-5081-0056-0 (pbk.) — ISBN 978-1-68048-309-3 (6-pack)
1. Green turtle—Juvenile literature. 2. Green turtle—Conservation—Juvenile literature. I. Title.

QL666.C536M33 2015
597.92'8--dc23

2015016638

Manufactured in the United States of America

Photo Credits: Cover David Carbo/Shutterstock.com; back cover, p. 1, interior pages background Rich Carey/Shutterstock.com; p. 4 Jolanta Wojcicka/Shutterstock.com; p. 5 Isabelle Kuehn/Shutterstock.com; p. 6 Heather Lucia Snow/Shutterstock.com; p. 7 hansgertbroeder/iStock/Thinkstock; p. 8 inge804/iStock/Thinkstock; p. 9 Dtamarack/iStock/Thinkstock; p. 10 neijia/Shutterstock.com; p. 11 Fiona Ayerst/Shutterstock.com; p. 12 stephan kerkhofs/Shutterstock.com; p. 13 pilesasmiles/iStock/Thinkstock; p. 14 David Evison/Shutterstock.com; p. 15 DEA/P.Jaccod/De Agostini/Getty Images; p. 16 Jason Edwards/National Geographic Image Collection/Getty Images; p. 17 Michael & Jennifer Lewis/National Geographic Image Collection/Getty Images; p. 18 MyLoupe/Universal Images Group/Getty Images; p. 19 Erik S. Lesser/Getty Images; p. 20 Three Lions/Hulton Archive/Getty Images; p. 21 Norm Diver/Shutterstock.com; p. 22 Antonio Ribeiro/iStock/Thinkstock; p. 23 Harry Thomas/iStock/Thinkstock; p. 24 Greg Wood/AFP/Getty Images; p. 25 Richard Ellis/Getty Images; p. 26 Rex Features/AP Images; p. 27 © AP Images; p. 28 © Howard Lipin /The U-T San Diego/ZUMA Press; p. 29 Al Seib/Los Angeles Times/Getty Images; cover and interior pages design elements Aliaksei_7799/Shutterstock.com (turtle graphic), jeep2499/Shutterstock.com (shell detail).

CONTENTS

UPSETTING THE BALANCE

The world's oceans are full of many types of plants and animals that have lived there for thousands of years. Those plants and animals together make up the ocean ecosystems. Although humans are usually far removed from these ecosystems, their activities often have a major effect on the

This beautiful coral reef is home to thousands of sea creatures, but it may not always be that way.

Vocabulary

Endangered is when a plant or animal is in danger of disappearing forever.

oceans. Fishing, building along coastlines, and dumping poisonous waste upset the health of the ocean ecosystems. Harmful chemicals can kill creatures or make them sick. Large fishing nets can catch other creatures by accident and cause them to suffer.

One animal that has been affected by human behavior is the green sea turtle. These creatures have been harmed so greatly that now they are **endangered**.

Because of the harmful behavior of humans, the green sea turtle has become endangered.

THE TURTLE FAMILY

These green sea turtles swam through the ocean and crawled onto the beach to lay their eggs.

Sea turtles are turtles that live in the oceans. There are seven species, or kinds, of sea turtles. Green sea turtles are one species. The others are leatherbacks, flatbacks, loggerheads, hawksbills, Kemp's ridleys, and olive ridleys. Like all turtles, sea turtles are reptiles. Reptiles are cold-blooded animals that have scales.

Sea turtles are great swimmers, thanks to their flippers and webbed feet. On land, their flippers and feet help them crawl and dig. Green sea turtles can stay underwater longer than any sea turtle. However, like all sea turtles, they need to breathe air. Green sea turtles may rest for up to five hours underwater before surfacing for air. They breathe more often when they are active.

The turtle's wide, flat flippers help it glide through water.

Compare and Contrast

Sea turtles have features that help them on land and features that help them in the water. Can you identify some of each?

WARM, WATERY WORLD

Green sea turtles live in the warm parts of the Atlantic, Pacific, and Indian oceans. They are commonly found near the coasts of Florida, the Caribbean islands, Costa Rica, and western Mexico. A large population of sea turtles lives around the Hawaiian Islands.

Tropical and sub-tropical waters are home to green sea turtle populations.

A green sea turtle can live to be about 100 years old. It does not stay in the same waters for its whole life. Young green sea turtles

Think About It

People travel the same waters and beaches as green sea turtles. How might this affect the turtles?

live far out in the open ocean. Adults prefer the shallow waters around coral reefs or along the coast.

During the mating season, adult green sea turtles travel long distances to return to the beaches where they were born. Females come ashore to dig nests in the sand and lay their eggs.

Green sea turtles like to swim around coral reefs.

TURTLE BODY

The color and markings on this turtle's shell and body show that it is a green sea turtle.

Green sea turtles are one of the largest sea turtle species. They can weigh up to 350 pounds (159 kilograms)! Green sea turtles are best known for their smooth, heart-shaped carapace, or shell. On average, the shells of adult green sea turtles measure between 3 and 4 feet (91 and 122 centimeters) long. The carapace top is bony, and its bottom is covered with scales.

Compare and Contrast

Many sea animals have flippers and webbed feet. How are they more useful for life in the water than the hands and feet of other animals?

A green sea turtle's color varies. Its carapace can be brown, dark olive, black, gray, or a mix of these colors. The belly is yellowish white. A green sea turtle's small head has brown and yellow markings. Flippers for front limbs and webbed hind feet help it swim.

The green sea turtle's belly isn't as colorful as the rest of its body. Front flippers help the turtle move through the water.

GIANT VEGETARIANS

If green sea turtles aren't aways green, where do they get their colorful name? It comes from the layer of fat underneath their skin. The fat has a green color because of the turtle's diet.

Green sea turtles eat mostly algae and sea grasses. Their mouths are shaped to help them eat plants. Their jaws are serrated, which means they have edges like a

A green sea turtle feasts on sea grass. This diet makes the fat under its skin green.

Think About It

Too much algae can kill corals, which in turn harms sea creatures that live along coral reefs. How does the green sea turtle keep its ecosystem among coral reefs balanced?

saw. This helps them cut sea grasses and scrape algae off of hard surfaces.

Unlike their parents, young green sea turtles eat both plants and animals. They eat sea grasses and seaweed, but they also eat small ocean creatures, such as insects, mollusks, crustaceans, and worms.

The turtle's saw-like jaw is much like a lawn mower—for grass under the sea!

TO THE BEACH

Sea turtles use their hind legs to dig nests for their eggs and their flippers to cover the eggs with sand.

Sea turtles are likely to be found on beaches in late spring and early summer. That's when their **mating** season occurs. Sea turtles migrate, or travel, across oceans to reach their nesting site, which is often the same beach where they were born.

All sea turtles lay eggs, including the green sea turtle. The females come ashore at night to dig a nest in the sand.

Vocabulary

Mating is the joining of a male and female to produce babies.

They dig their nest with their hind legs. After they lay their eggs, they use their front flippers to cover the nest with sand. Then they return to the water.

Sea turtle nests are called clutches, and a female may make several of them in one nesting season. A clutch may contain 100 to 200 eggs—that's a lot of turtles!

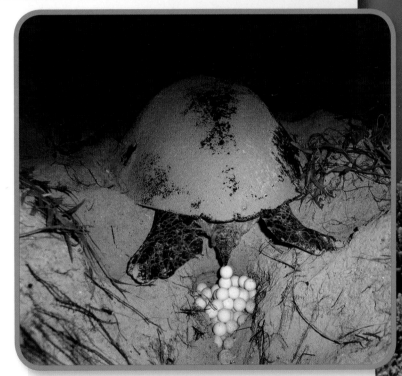

This is just one of many clutches that green sea turtles laid on a beach in Australia. Each clutch may contain more than 100 future turtles.

TO THE SEA

After the female turtle returns to the sea, her eggs incubate in the nest for about sixty days. Turtle eggs are buried deep in the sand. When the turtles hatch, the young, called hatchlings, work together to dig up and out of the nest in the sand. Then they must make their way to the water and swim out to sea.

A hatchling breaks out of its egg. This young sea turtle has a big journey ahead of it.

Think About It

For every 1,000 hatchlings, about one will survive to adulthood. How does this affect the world's sea turtle population?

This is the most dangerous part of a turtle's life. If they do not make it to the water, they die. Many animals, including crabs and birds, prey on hatchlings. Once the hatchlings are in the water, sharks or fish may eat them. They can also die from swallowing plastic or trash that has been tossed in the ocean.

It's a race to the water once the hatchlings emerge from their shells. Making it to the water is essential for the turtle's survival.

HATCHLINGS AT RISK

Disturbing green sea turtles as they lay their eggs may have harmful effects on the already endangered species.

Baby sea turtles hatch at night, but they are naturally attracted to light. They use the moon's reflection on the water to guide them to the sea.

As people continue to develop beaches, sea turtles are put at risk. Light pollution confuses hatchlings. Bright lights from hotels, restaurants, and shops may cause the hatchlings to move the wrong way. Also, beaches occupied by

Compare and Contrast

Developing beaches hurts sea turtles, but people living near beaches can step in to help them. Compare and contrast how people both harm and help turtles.

humans do not have space for female turtles to dig nests.

Disturbing sea turtles' nesting areas hurts this species' ability to survive. People can help by shutting down stretches of beaches during turtle nesting season. That is one way to make sure new generations of sea turtles develop safely.

DO NOT DISTURB

SEA TURTLE NEST

VIOLATORS SUBJECT TO FINES AND IMPRISONMENT

FLORIDA LAW CHAPTER 370

No person may take, possess, disturb, mutilate, destroy, cause to be destroyed, sell, offer for sale, transfer, molest, or harass any marine turtle nest or eggs at any time.

Upon conviction, a person may be imprisoned for a period of up to 60 days or fined up to $500, or both, plus an additional penalty of $100 for each sea turtle egg destroyed or taken.

U.S. ENDANGERED SPECIES ACT OF 1973

No person may take, harass, harm, pursue, hunt, shoot, wound, kill, trap, or capture any marine turtle, turtle nest, and/or eggs, or attempt to engage in any such conduct.

Any person who knowingly violates any provision of this act may be assessed a civil penalty up to $25,000 or a criminal penalty up to $100,000 and up to one year imprisonment.

SHOULD YOU WITNESS A VIOLATION, OBSERVE AN INJURED OR STRANDED TURTLE, OR MISORIENTED HATCHLINGS, PLEASE CONTACT FLORIDA MARINE PATROL AT 1-800-DIAL-FMP

FLORIDA FISH AND WILDLIFE CONSERVATION COMMISSION MARINE TURTLE PROTECTION PROGRAM

COASTLINE 904-761-1414

Warning signs such as this one have helped keep sea turtles—and their nests—safe from people.

HARMFUL HUMANS

Even if sea turtles survive the first few years of life, they are still in danger. People have hunted green sea turtles since the 1500s. They capture the eggs or the turtles themselves for food. They also use the shells for jewelry and for other decorative items. Over-hunting has reduced the number of green sea turtles in the

Hunters have harmed the world's green sea turtle population.

Think About It

People are sea turtles' greatest threat. How can people change their behavior to stop harming sea turtles and other ocean creatures?

world's oceans from millions to thousands.

Some sea turtles are captured accidentally when they get caught in fishing nets. Others are harmed by boat propellers or when they eat fishing lines, plastic bags, and other items people throw into the sea. Human activity invades the habitat of the sea turtle and threatens its survival.

When sea turtles get caught in fishing nets, there is little they can do to get free. Be aware of what you throw into the ocean!

A CHANGING PLANET

As the planet's ice melts, the homes of thousands of sea creatures change forever.

Sea turtles have been on Earth for more than 100 million years. Over time, their bodies adapted to environmental changes in order to survive. However, the planet's climate has changed greatly in the last 100 years. This change is hurting the turtles and their habitats.

Climate change is a huge threat to all sea turtles. As the planet warms, large

Vocabulary

Climate change is a change in Earth's climate because of high levels of carbon dioxide trapped in the atmosphere, which is caused by burning fossil fuels.

areas of ice called glaciers melt. This causes sea levels to rise and cover the beaches where sea turtles nest. Higher temperatures can cause sea turtle eggs to hatch before they're fully developed or not to hatch at all. Warmer temperatures in the ocean may kill corals, which are an essential part of the ecosystems of many sea turtles.

Beaches used for nesting have been covered by rising sea levels. Having no place to lay their eggs threatens the sea turtle population.

EXPERT HELP

Tagging allows scientists to track the activities of sea turtles in the water and on land.

Human behavior and a changing climate have harmed green sea turtles so much that they have become endangered. In fact, a population in the Mediterranean Sea is considered **critically endangered**. Without action, we risk losing these creatures forever.

Scientists and conservationists around the world are working to help sea turtles. Many conservation groups monitor sea

Vocabulary

Critically endangered means a species is facing an extremely high risk of extinction, or dying out permanently.

turtles' behavior and migration patterns. They keep track of their population numbers and breeding patterns, too.

An important conservation effort is protecting sea turtles' nesting habitats. Conservation groups have worked to get stretches of beaches shut down during nesting season. They've also tried to stop companies from developing on and near beaches. A group called the Sea Turtle Conservancy has designed turtle-friendly lights that can be used safely around water without confusing hatchlings.

This sea turtle was rescued and taken to a rehabilitation facility before being released back into the wild.

RAISING AWARENESS

Conservation groups have worked hard to get governments to pass laws that protect green sea turtles from being hunted for their meat, eggs, and shells. Conservation efforts have also led to a change in fishing practices. Today, many fishing companies use gear that allows turtles to escape if they get caught in nets. There are also efforts to close

This turtle was found tangled in a net. Luckily, it was rescued, brought back to health, and returned to the water.

Think About It

What can individuals do to make more people aware of the threat to green sea turtles?

areas of water to fishing boats during nesting and hatching season.

Conservation groups such as the World Wildlife Fund and the National Wildlife Federation also raise awareness about how human behavior is affecting the world's plant and animal life. By knowing the source of the problem, we have a better chance of fixing it.

Conservation groups are working to save the green sea turtle from extinction.

YOU CAN HELP!

These students get a chance to see young sea turtles up close.

You are never too young to help sea turtles. You can start by reaching out to conservation groups in your area. They have experts who can come to your school to talk about sea turtles, or they can send you more information. In coastal areas, conservation groups get together to clean up beaches. You can also choose not to buy or use products that come from hunted turtles.

Think About It
How does litter on beaches hurt green sea turtles?

One of the best ways to help sea turtles is to think about the impact that you have on the environment. Recycle whenever you can and remember not to litter. Talk to your family about ways you can keep our planet safe and clean for all living creatures. With your help, sea turtles may no longer be endangered one day.

Keeping our beaches clean is an easy and important way we can help sea turtles.

GLOSSARY

ADAPT To adjust to new conditions.

BREED To produce offspring.

CLIMATE The average weather conditions in an area over time.

CONSERVATIONIST Someone who works to protect nature.

CRUSTACEAN An animal, such as a crab, shrimp, or lobster, that usually has a hard covering, or exoskeleton, and two pairs of antennas, or feelers.

ECOSYSTEM The living and nonliving things that exist together in one place.

IMPACT The effect or influence of one thing on another.

INCUBATE To keep eggs at a suitable temperature so that they develop and hatch.

LIGHT POLLUTION Brightening of the sky caused by street lights and other man-made light sources.

MIGRATE To move from one region or habitat to another.

MOLLUSK An invertebrate that belongs to a group that includes snails, slugs, mussels, and octopuses.

POLLUTION The dirtying of air, water, or land.

RECYCLE To convert waste into reusable materials.

SHALLOW Not deep.

TEMPERATURE A measurement that tells how hot or cold something is.

THREAT Danger.

Books

Gagne, Tammy. *The Most Endangered Animals in the World*. North Mankato, MN: Capstone Press, 2015.

Hirsch, Rebecca E. *Green Sea Turtle Migration*. Mankato, MN: The Child's World, 2012.

Jackson, Tom. *Green Sea Turtle*.New York, NY: Bearport Publishing, 2014.

Marsh, Laura. *Sea Turtles*. Des Moines, IA: National Geographic Children's Books, 2011.

Spilsbury, Louise. *Sea Turtles*. Portsmouth, NH: Heinemann Publishing, 2010.

Websites

Because of the changing nature of Internet links, Rosen Publishing has developed an online list of websites related to the subject of this book. This site is updated regularly. Please use this link to access the list:

http://www.rosenlinks.com/CONS/Turtle

INDEX